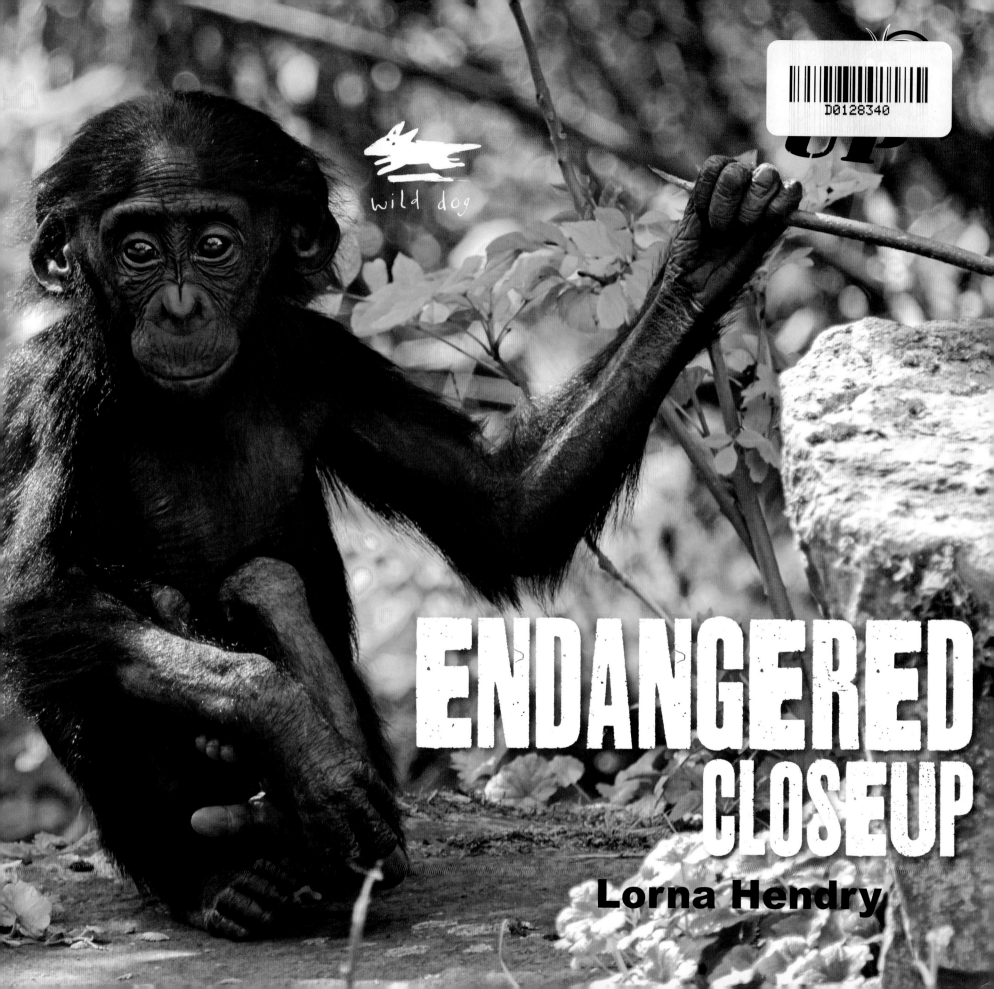

wild dog

ENDANGERED
CLOSEUP
Lorna Hendry

ORANGUTANS are apes that live in Borneo and Sumatra. They are endangered because the rainforests where they live are being destroyed, making it hard for them to find food. They are also captured and sold as pets. Wildlife organizations rescue orangutans and release them into protected areas where they will be safe.

PRZEWALSKI'S HORSES are the only true wild horses in the world. They have never been tamed. They once roamed the plains of Mongolia, but were hunted for their meat. Fifty years ago there were none left in the wild.

Now, after being bred in captivity, there are 1800 Przewalski's Horses, and 300 live in the wild.

TIGERS are the largest cats in the world. There are fewer than 4000 left. People are cutting down the forests where they live and hunting them for their skins. A worldwide campaign aims to increase their numbers in the next decade.

CALIFORNIA CONDORS are one of the largest birds in North America. They are dying out because the places where they live are being destroyed. Some die of lead poisoning after eating dead animals that have been shot with lead bullets.

When there were only 22 left in the wild, they were all put in zoos to keep them safe. Now there are more than 400 birds and more than half are back in the wild.

GIANT PANDAS are bears that live in China. Pandas mainly eat bamboo, and they need a lot of it to survive. Most of the forests where they live are being destroyed by logging, farming, and mining. There are about 2000 pandas left. Reserves have been set up to look after them.

TASMANIAN DEVILS are only the size of a small dog but they look and sound very fierce. They are threatened by a rare cancer that gives them sores and lumps around their face and makes it hard for them to eat.

Healthy Tasmanian Devils are being looked after in reserves in case the wild population dies out.

HAWKSBILL SEA TURTLES have a curved beak like a bird. The adults live much of the time in shallow lagoons and on coral reefs. Young turtles live in the open ocean.

Turtles are endangered because people hunt them for their shells and meat, and collect and eat their eggs. Some turtles die because they accidentally swallow plastic bags, which can look like jellyfish.

BLACK RHINOCEROSES live in Africa. People hunt them for their horns, which are made into handles for daggers or ground up and used as medicine. There are fewer than 5000 left. They all live in wildlife reserves.

ADDAX are a type of large antelope. They are endangered because they are hunted for their meat and skins.

Today there are fewer than 300 addax in the wild, over 600 in captive breeding programs, and more than 1000 in private collections.

AMUR LEOPARDS are found in parts of Russia and China. In recent years their numbers in the wild have dropped below 30, as they are threatened by hunters and loss of habitat. A campaign aims to increase the number of wild Amur leopards to 160 in the coming years.

SEA OTTERS rely on their thick fur coat to stay warm. Their fur was once so valuable they were nearly hunted to extinction.

Now one of the greatest threats to sea otters is oil pollution. When their fur is covered in oil, they can die from becoming too cold.

SLOW LORISES live in South and South-East Asia. Some species are threatened because much of the forests where they live are being destroyed. They are also hunted and then sold as pets.

It is not just large animals that are endangered — lots of insects are too! Some types of bee are becoming extinct because of pesticides and because the places where they live are being destroyed.

BEES are very important to the environment. They help fertilize plants by moving pollen from one flower to another.

Animals can be helped saved from becoming extinct by creating national parks, wildlife sanctuaries, and reserves, where they can be protected.

ELEPHANTS are a threatened species. This means they are at risk of becoming endangered. Threatened species are also protected in parks and reserves.

People all over the world are working hard to help endangered animals.

You can help too, by finding out more about these animals and how we can make the Earth a better place to live.

First published in 2013 by
wild dog
54A Alexandra Parade
Clifton Hill Vic 3068
Australia
+61 3 9419 9406
dog@wdog.com.au
wdog.com.au

This edition published in 2014

Printed and bound in China by Everbest Printing Co. Ltd

Distributed in the U.S.A. by
Scholastic Inc.
New York, NY 10012

ISBN: 978-174203313-6 (pbk)

10 9 8 7 6 5 4 3 2 1   14 15 16 17 18

PHOTO CREDITS:
All images courtesy of Shutterstock.
Front cover Hung Chung Chih; p. 1 EBFoto; pp. 2-3 Nagel Photography; pp. 4-5 llaszlo; pp. 6-7 Jackiso; pp. 8-9 kojihirano; pp. 10-11 Hung Chung Chih; pp. 12-13 Flash-ka; pp. 14-15 Rich Carey; pp. 16-17 Johan Swanepoel; pp. 18-19 ChameleonsEye; pp. 20-21 Dmitri Gomon; pp. 22-23 worldswildlifewonders; pp. 24-25 nattanan726; pp. 26-27 johannviloria; pp. 28-29 Graeme Shannon; p. 30 A. S. Zain; p. 31 MarcelClemens; p. 32 Eric Isselee; Back cover SasinT.

Wild Dog would like to thank Doug Robinson and Neil Conning for their factual checks of this book. The numbers quoted in this book are taken from the International Union for Conservation of Nature (IUCN) website: www.iucn.org.

GLOSSARY:

ENDANGERED ANIMAL: An animal that is at risk of becoming extinct.

EXTINCT: No longer existing, died out.

LOGGING: Cutting down trees and forests.

POLLUTION: Anything that makes the air, land, or sea dirty.

PROTECTED: Making it against the law to hunt or hurt an animal.

RESERVES AND SANCTUARIES: Places where animals are protected.

THREATENED ANIMAL: An animal that is at risk of becoming endangered.